LaMarcus Aldridge: The Inspiring Story of One of Basketball's Most Dominant Power Forwards

An Unauthorized Biography

By: Clayton Geoffreys

Table of Contents

Foreword

One free agent demanded the attention of practically any team with salary cap room in the summer of 2015. That free agent was LaMarcus Aldridge. Since entering the league, LaMarcus Aldridge has established himself as one of the premier power forwards to play professional basketball today. With a unique ability to stretch the floor, Aldridge poses a significant offensive threat to any opposing defense. Since joining the San Antonio Spurs in the 2015 offseason, LaMarcus has gelled quickly to become part of the future of the organization alongside Kawhi Leonard. Thank you for purchasing *LaMarcus Aldridge: The Inspiring Story of One of Basketball's Most Dominant Power Forwards*. In this unauthorized biography, we will learn LaMarcus' incredible life story and impact on the game of basketball. Hope you enjoy and if you do, please do not forget to leave a review!

Also, check out my website at claytongeoffreys.com to join my exclusive list where I let you know about my latest books. To thank you for your purchase, you can go to my site to download a free copy of *33 Life Lessons: Success Principles, Career Advice & Habits of Successful People*. In the book, you'll learn from some of the greatest thought leaders of different industries on what it takes to become successful and how to live a great life.

Cheers,

Clayton Geoffreys

Visit me at www.claytongeoffreys.com

Introduction

To be one of the best power forwards in the modern-day NBA, the player must possess the perfect combination of size, length, and skill. Among the many power forwards in this generation, a few come to mind whenever you think of those qualities. One such power forward is LaMarcus Aldridge. Standing at 6'11" with wingspan of almost 7'5", LaMarcus Aldridge, a.k.a. LA, has the size and length needed for an elite power forward to excel in the NBA. LA is also one of the more offensively skilled 4's in the world. Aldridge earns his millions by camping out in the perimeter and making mid-range jump shots all day long. Despite his penchant for shooting jumpers from the perimeter, Aldridge is also a skilled player down at the post. He can bang with the best power forwards on the low block using his size and has an array of post moves, especially his go-to-move, the turnaround jump shot.

LaMarcus Aldridge's talent and abilities have contributed to his success in the NBA. Aldridge has been an All-Star four times from 2012 up until 2015. He has also been named as one of the best players in the NBA, was an All-NBA Second Team member in 2015, and was a two-time All-NBA Third Team selection in 2011 and in 2014. Individual accomplishments don't give justice to the kind of player that LA is. Aside from garnering player accolades, he has also led the Portland Trailblazers to five NBA playoff appearances and has always made the Blazers good enough to do some damage in the postseason. LA has also been a perennial pick for the Team USA Select Team because of how well he could play the match-up nightmare against international competition with his combination of size and skillful play out in the perimeter.

When Aldridge was playing for the Portland Trailblazers, he was undoubtedly the best player on the team. When the Blazers were suffering injury setbacks with former top players Brandon Roy and Greg Oden, LA picked up the pieces needed to push the Blazers to playoff contention. When Roy and Oden left the team and the game of basketball for good, LA became the first option on offense for the Trailblazers and became a virtual 20-10 guy every night. In his nine seasons with the Portland Trailblazers, LaMarcus Aldridge averaged 19.3 points per game and 8.4 rebounds per game. In only nine seasons with the Blazers, LA has become the second leading scorer in the team's history with a total of 12,562, and also its leading rebounder with 5434 rebounds. With his length, LaMarcus has also become the fourth highest shot blocker in Blazers history.

When Aldridge left the Blazers for free agency in 2015, he quickly became the top free agent in the market. Many teams were highly interested in the All-Star power forward including the San Antonio Spurs, the Los Angeles Lakers, the Houston Rockets, the Phoenix Suns, and the Dallas Mavericks, his hometown team.[i]

His top stock in free agency is proof of how he is regarded as one of the top, if not the best, power forwards in today's league. In the end he chose, and is currently playing for, the San Antonio Spurs. LaMarcus Aldridge has further strengthened the already ultra-strong Spurs lineup. Aldridge now plays together in the frontcourt with arguably the best power forward in history and his longtime idol, Tim Duncan. Now learning with one of the greatest and at the peak of his career, there's no telling how much better and how much more accomplished Aldridge will be in years to come.

Chapter 1: Aldridge's Early Life and Childhood

LaMarcus Nurae Aldridge was born on July 19, 1985 in Dallas, Texas. LA's parents, Marvin and Georgia Aldridge, are tall people in their own right. Marvin, who also played a lot of basketball, stands at 6'6" while Georgia is 6'2".[ii] With genetics in play, one can understand how LaMarcus came to be so tall and long at the peak of his growth. Aldridge has an older brother LaVontae who is six years his senior. LaVontae also benefited from his parents' genetics and currently stands at 6'10". LaVontae was a very good basketball player in high school and played well in college.[iii]

Though basketball ran in the family bloodline, LaMarcus did not love the sport at first sight. LA first enjoyed the sport of football, having rooted for the Dallas Cowboys for as far back as he can remember. Over time, LA learned to play and love the sport of basketball. It was in fourth grade when LaMarcus Aldridge would first get to play basketball. However, basketball was not an easy thing to do for the young LA. He was so bad at it that he was often useless and picked as the last team member in ballpark pick-up games. His usual role was just to stand up on the court and pass the ball around if it ever found its way to him. He had no offensive moves in the post and he could not shoot jump shots.

In later years when LaMarcus grew into his body, he was taller than everyone else. Despite his size and length, he was still awful at basketball. He did not have unique moves inside the paint, and the only reason he could score was that he was taller than anyone else.[iv] In 8th grade, LaMarcus was standing at a ridiculous height of 6'7". His height was all that he had, though. He did not have the skills or the makings of a future NBA player at all, much less an All-Star with the league. A lot of the league's best power forwards like Kevin Garnett and Tim Duncan were instant basketball prodigies when they were in 8th grade. Aldridge was different. He was awkward with the basketball.

The worst part of it all was that Marvin Aldridge was not very supportive of his family, nor of his children. He had a very bad drinking problem and would rather buy booze and alcohol than pay for the family's welfare to the point that they were always tardy in paying for the bills. In the end, Georgia kicked the delinquent father out of the Aldridge household when LaMarcus was in the middle of his childhood. Without his father, LA was without a father figure and a person to help him with basketball. Though his father was not a big part in his life, LaMarcus inherited Marvin's good basketball pedigree. That was the least LA's father could do for his career. And even though the Aldridge family struggled as a one-parent household, Georgia did all that she could to support her sons' basketball career.

LaMarcus turned to his brother for help and advice. LaVontae was a terrific high school player and was always a hardworking fellow in terms of improving his game. He instilled the same hardworking attitude in his younger brother LaMarcus. He pushed and told LA to work on his game every single day and to never let up when it came to any opportunity to get better.[v] When LaVontae went on to play college basketball, LaMarcus was already good enough to play varsity in high school and was gaining confidence in his abilities. LaMarcus Aldridge became an instant star in high school, thanks in part to his brother, who helped him to become a good player early in his life.

Chapter 2: LaMarcus Aldridge's High School Career

LaMarcus Aldridge enrolled in Seagoville High School in the year 2000. At that time, he already showed early flashes of brilliance and had a lot of skill for a kid at his age. He could already hit jump shots and had the footwork down at the low post good enough for inside moves. LA was a far cry from the 6'7" kid in middle school who could not even hit jumpers and hook shots. Indeed, his hard work a few years ago had paid off well.

The best part about high school for LaMarcus Aldridge was his coach Robert Allen, who he credits as the most influential person in his growth as a basketball player. LA said that Allen worked tirelessly on him and pushed his stamina and endurance to their very limit during his whole high school career.[vi] Allen would make LA run almost nine miles every time his star player was lazy in practice.[vii] Allen knew that he had a gem in Aldridge and wanted the young boy to realize his potential.

With Allen's hard work on Aldridge and with his tutelage, Aldridge became a high school basketball phenom by the time he reached his second year in high school and earned second team all-state and second team all-district.[viii] LA was literally the first person to come into the gym and the last person to leave. He would watch films of basketball rivals such as Chris Bosh, who played for another Dallas high school, to learn their tendencies and their team's strategies. Even when the power was out, Allen said that Aldridge would still play late at night with only the stars to light up the gym.

In what was one of the highlights of his sophomore year in Seagoville, Aldridge faced Chris Bosh, who would later become an NBA All-Star. Bosh was just as good of a player as Aldridge was, and both players were comparable in terms of skillset, size, and length. Aldridge got the best of Bosh in that game by recording 22 points and 12 rebounds while Chris only had 18 and 10. Bosh, however, won the team game by beating Seagoville in a blowout fashion. In the two games that Aldridge played with Bosh in high school, he averaged 23 points and 13 rebounds.

In Aldridge's junior year in high school, he was even more dominant. Aldridge was first team all-state and first team all-district. He was literally and figuratively the biggest star basketball player in the Lone Star State of Texas. He averaged 27 points per game, 13.4 rebounds per game, and swatted 4 shots per game. After a stellar junior year, LA was chosen as one of the players to represent the Team USA for the FIBA Junior World Championships.

LaMarcus continued to become one of the best stars in Texas in his senior year. He also continued his improvement as a player. Aside from winning numerous first team selections the same way he had done the previous years, Aldridge was a McDonald's All-American and averaged nearly 30 points per game and 14 rebounds per game. Aldridge was also responsible for leading Seagoville to the state tournament quarterfinals, but eventually lost. The highlight of his high school senior year, however, was not about basketball. In his final year, he was the best scholar-athlete in the state of Texas as an honor student. At the end of his senior year, he was ranked as the fourth best high school player in America and was, academically, one of the top performing high school athletes. At that time, he was already good enough to get himself drafted into the NBA but needed more polishing to become a promising future star.

Chapter 3: LaMarcus Aldridge's College Career

Freshman Year

LaMarcus Aldridge originally intended to join the NBA Draft in 2004. Numerous scouts pegged him to be a lottery pick or, at the very least, within the top 20. However, LaMarcus Aldridge was suffering from a stress fracture in his back. Since many NBA teams tend to be wary about injury-prone players despite their talents, Aldridge feared that he might drop to the second round if he continued with the draft. He did not want to waste his basketball career as a second round draft pick that has no guaranteed chance at an NBA contract. Because of that, LA accepted the scholarship offered to him by the University of Texas.

Aldridge was a good player as a freshman at the University of Texas. He was an instant starter after Rick Barnes saw the young power forward's work ethic and potential to be a star. He was playing well alongside two other All-Americans Daniel Gibson and Mike Williams. With him as a starter, the Longhorns were competitive enough in the Big 12 Conference. He was not the best player or the top scorer on the floor, but he provided good presence inside with his rebounding and defense.

The worse came for Aldridge and the Texas Longhorns when, in the 16th game of the season, LA suffered a season-ending hip injury. The injury caused him to miss the next 15 games and the Longhorns did not even make the NCAA Tournament without their starting big man. In his freshman season, LaMarcus Aldridge averaged 9.9 points and 5.9 rebounds while playing only 22.2 minutes in 16 games. If he had been healthy the entire year, Aldridge would have played better and would have led his team to an appearance at the NCAA Tournament. Aldridge may have been able to skip the next year in college to go straight to the NBA had he not suffered the injury he did in his freshman year. The injury turned out to be a blessing in disguise, though, as it gave him another opportunity and one more year to gain confidence as a star and to improve his skills as a power forward on the rise.

After suffering the season-ending injury, Aldridge had surgery to fix his injured hip. He could not use much of his lower body after the surgery. With his work ethic, Aldridge could not resist improving his game. Because of that, LA spent tons of hours in the weight room to strengthen his upper body. He bulked up his physique and made sure he could still shoot jump shots solely on the strength of his upper body. It was because of the work he put in during his injury that he was able to shoot jumpers by using more of his upper body than his lower body. This would prove to be a solid weapon for Aldridge since he could still shoot jump shots late into the game when the legs started to get tired.

One other thing that he and his coach Rick Barnes worked on was his fadeaway jump shot. They used two players as models for Aldridge's own fadeaway—Tim Duncan and Rasheed Wallace. Barnes and Aldridge would watch videos of Duncan and Wallace to break down and study the way they shot their jump shots. Barnes helped his young player in retooling his shot and had him release it much higher than he usually did, similar to how Tim and Rasheed did. LaMarcus worked on his shot by shooting from a chair over and over again while he was injured. Again, he was using more of his upper body than his legs in shooting jump shots. LA did this routine for hours a day for two months and later moved outside to the three-point line.[ix]

Sophomore Year

The way Aldridge worked on his shot when he was injured was what really helped him become the college star (and later NBA All-Star) that he was. His high release was deadly especially because Aldridge was so much taller and longer than most other big men in college. Thus, he was the uncontested go-to-guy for the Texas Longhorns and led the team in scoring and intangibles.

LaMarcus had other elite teammates on his team. The Texas Longhorns had forward PJ Tucker, who now plays for the Phoenix Suns, and also guard Daniel Gibson, who played his best years alongside LeBron James in the King's first go-around with Cleveland. Aldridge and Tucker were the best rebounding duo of forwards in the Big 12 that season. Aldridge also dominated the other Big 12's big men. He earned Defensive Player of the Year in the Big 12 in 2006 and was also in the All-Defensive First Team and the First Team All-Big 12. Aldridge and the Longhorns dominated the conference with 30 wins and only 7 losses. He was unquestionably the most dominant player in the Big 12 that year on both offense and defense.

The strength of the Texas lineup and the leadership of LaMarcus propelled the Longhorns to the NCAA

Tournament where they reached as far as the Elite Eight. However, they were beaten by LSU in that stage of the tournament and failed to reach the Final Four. LSU was led by lottery prospect Tyrus Thomas who would later play a big, albeit indirect, role in LA's NBA career. According to Barnes, Aldridge was upset about losing to LSU because he worked so hard every day just to win games. He was just so unselfish that way and wanted his team to win despite knowing he would be coming over to the NBA after the NCAA season.[x]

At the end of the season, he averaged 15.9 points and 9.2 rebounds. The National Association of Basketball Coaches (NABC) named Aldridge as a member of the All-American Third Team. Similar to his high school career, LA was also one of the best student-athletes in Texas. He was a steady A and B student even while he was working hard on his basketball game and leading the Longhorns to the NCAA tournament.

At the end of his sophomore year with the University of Texas Longhorns, LaMarcus Aldridge decided to go pro along with teammates Daniel Gibson and PJ Tucker. With all his prep and college accomplishments, LA was one of the best prospects in the entire country and draft class. He was a shoe-in for the lottery and some even put him at the top of the first five picks. He was also pegged as the best big man in his draft class along with highly touted Italian big man Andrea Bargnani. Indeed, Aldridge was one of the best in his draft class, if not the best, judging by how great his NBA career has been.

Chapter 4: LaMarcus Aldridge's NBA Career

Getting Drafted

Aldridge was one of the best prospects in the 2006 NBA Draft because of how accomplished he was in college and in leading the Texas Longhorns. Aldridge was a true power forward in every sense of the position. He stood an inch shy of being 7 feet tall and was one of the few college players that already had an NBA-ready body at 245 lbs. of lean muscle mass. More impressive was how long he was. LaMarcus Aldridge had a wingspan as wide as Yao Ming. Despite his height and size, Aldridge was a very mobile big man who could move quickly, cover the perimeter, and jump up to block shots. His skills and his physical attributes propelled him to a possible top five pick in the 2006 NBA Draft, and perhaps even the first overall pick.

Because of his size and skillset, NBA scouts often compared LaMarcus Aldridge at his best to Kevin Garnett. At his worst, Aldridge was more comparable to Channing Frye. He was compared to such players because he had a similar length and a similar tendency to shoot jump shots. Nevertheless, Aldridge was one prospect any NBA team would have been happy to draft and develop into a star player like Kevin Garnett or into a capable role player like Channing Frye.

LaMarcus Aldridge was considered to be the top big man in his draft class. On offense, Aldridge had a smooth-looking jump shot that could extend anywhere within the three-point line. LA shot his jump shots so high above his head and had such an incredibly long wingspan that it was virtually impossible to block his jump shots unless the defender could jump 60 inches off the ground or stood 8-feet tall. He also had a well-refined post game that could help him dominate smaller power forwards. He could shoot hook shots over his right shoulder and release it high enough above his head that it became very tough to guard. His go-to move at the post was always his turnaround jumper off the spin, or off a turn going to the left.[xi]

Not too many big men in the league can shoot from the perimeter and also get post-up baskets. This meant that Aldridge's skills were a premium in the league. One other strength that LA had was that he could score one on one. While most perimeter big men score on catch and shoot situations, LaMarcus could take his man off the dribble to pull up shots from 15-20 feet away from the basket. And despite heavy defense, he could shoot right over his man because of his length. He could also drive to the rim when he turned the corner. With his very long strides, he could easily get to the basket before the defense could even react.[xii]

Defensively, Aldridge was not a pushover. He always had a length good enough to get his hands on passing lanes for steals. LA could also jump high enough to swat shots with his long arms. His strongest defensive ability was his excellent ability to block shots on the ball instead of blocking from the help or the weak side. Rebounding-wise, LaMarcus was good in positioning for the boards. Though he was not a standout at that end of the floor, Aldridge was not a liability either and could develop into an excellent defender with time and effort.[xiii]

Even though Aldridge had an NBA-ready physique, he was never very physical, especially down at the low block. He was never as tough as big men his size or even as tough as smaller forwards. When scoring, LA always relied on his finesse and grace instead of getting physical or banging inside. With his fundamental skills, Aldridge never needed to get physical. The only time LA was reported to get physical was when he had a clear-cut size advantage over his defender. Other than that, he would just try to use his fundamentals to score.

LaMarcus was not well-known as a very good passer from the post. He never worked on that part of his game, despite being tall and long enough to see over the top of defenses to make plays for teammates. It would have been very good if he had developed his passing skills because he would later be double-teamed in the NBA if ever he got mismatches on the low block. Athletically, he was neither the highest leaper nor the fastest runner, though he had good mobility for his size. His ball handling also needed a lot of work, but that was never a skill required of men his size.

On the defensive side, Aldridge did not utilize enough of his size and length to rebound. Though he was good at positioning, he did not put the best effort in getting the boards. Similar to his offense, Aldridge got into trouble whenever his opponent got too physical on the low post. When the opposing player got too physical, especially with drop steps, LA tended to get pushed around and the opponent got easy baskets. For his size, LaMarcus shouldn't have even allowed himself to be bullied down at the post. Hence, his post defense needed a lot of work, and he always had trouble with the best post players. While he could block shots well,

LA didn't swat a lot of shots from the weak side because he did not help a lot on defense. He was usually content with just being able to defend his man one-on-one instead of actually beating him to the spot.[xiv] Nevertheless, Aldridge was too good of an offensive prospect to pass on, despite having a few weaknesses of his own. Defense and toughness are things players can be easily taught. However, when a player is as offensively gifted as LaMarcus has always been, you can easily disregard the weaknesses in the hopes of being able to develop the player defensively and physically.

On Draft night, the Toronto Raptors had the first overall pick. The 2006 Draft was interesting because nobody was the consensus top overall pick. Every scout and NBA analyst had their own top pick, but it all boiled down to what each team needed at the time.[xv] Several other players were highly touted like Adam Morrison, JJ Barea, and Rudy Gay. None of them had the upside that Aldridge had, though.

In the case of the Toronto Raptors, they already had Chris Bosh who was arguably their best player at that time and was developing into one of the best power forwards in the NBA. Bosh wanted the Raptors to draft Aldridge, who he knew since high school because of their legendary battles in Dallas. Despite actually contemplating drafting LA, the Raptors wanted a center because their power forward spot already belonged to Bosh. Hence, they went on to draft Italian 7-foot center Andrea Bargnani. This would prove to be an unwise choice because Bargnani never developed into an All-Star or even a game changer. Though Bargnani was a very good offensive player with his deft shooting touch from the outside, he was not the best defender and was a very poor rebounder despite his size.[xvi] He was, at best, a good role-playing starter because of his ability to space the floor with his jump shot. Had Toronto chosen Aldridge over Bargnani, they may have been a top contender for years to come and may not have lost Bosh go to free agency in 2010.

The Chicago Bulls were next on the block with the second overall pick. The Bulls wanted to take a power forward and contemplated between Aldridge and Tyrus Thomas from LSU, the team that eliminated LA's Longhorns in the NCAA. Chicago went on to draft the highly touted big man out of Texas University because he was the best available big man in the draft. Quickly enough, the Portland Trailblazers offered the Chicago Bulls a chance to get Tyrus Thomas with the fourth pick along with bench player Viktor Khryapa. The Chicago Bulls, unfortunately for them, bought the trade and ended up shipping Aldridge over to Portland. In a matter of minutes into his NBA career, LA was technically already a member of two different teams. In the end, he was going over to the Portland Trailblazers via a trade. The move for the Bulls would end up to be a bad one for them. The trade would look very one-sided if judged today because Tyrus Thomas has not even been seen around the NBA in recent seasons. In his best years, Thomas became a good defender but suddenly lost his way in the league. Meanwhile, LaMarcus Aldridge turned out well and developed to be one of the best power forwards in today's game.

Rookie Season

LaMarcus Aldridge, together with fellow rookie guard Brandon Roy, who was the sixth pick of the 2006 Draft, joined a Portland Trailblazers team that had struggled to make it into the playoffs for 4 years. The Blazers won a mere 21 games the previous year, but things looked bright for them with the addition of Aldridge and Roy into the lineup. Aldridge was promising, especially during the Summer League. His work ethic greatly impressed Blazers assistant coach Bill Bayno. Bayno believed that Aldridge had what it took to be an All-Star in the league, especially with his matured offense and growing defensive game.[xvii] The bad part for Coach Nate McMillan and his team was that their prized rookie, LA, suffered a shoulder injury in the ensuing months after the Summer League and prior to the start of the NBA season.

The injury sidelined LA till Portland's sixth game of the 2006-07 NBA season. When LA returned, he could not find his way into the starting lineup. The veteran and more established power forward, Zach Randolph, was starting and was dominating as power forward for the Blazers while McMillan opted to rotate Jamaal Magloire and Joel Pryzbilla at the center position. Hence, Aldridge would usually come off the bench as the backup for Randolph or as a center. Meanwhile, his fellow rookie Brandon Roy immediately found his way into the starting lineup due his terrific play and due to the Blazer's lack of depth in the two-guard position. Through his first set of games, Aldridge did not disappoint as he averaged about 8 points per game while making half of his shots.

What would become one of the highlights of his rookie season was when he was asked to match up with Tim Duncan, one of his childhood idols. Aldridge played

Duncan well and actually made scoring a little difficult for the two-time MVP. What made life difficult for Duncan was that LA was so long to the point that he could not easily make his usual shots over the rookie's outstretched arms. Though the Blazers lost that game against San Antonio, Aldridge was able to play well against his longtime hero and the player that would soon be his teammate and mentor. He played so well that Duncan could not help but compliment the rookie power forward after the game.[xviii]

Matched-up with another legendary power forward, Aldridge played more than what he was required to when he defended Dirk Nowitzki in a game against the Dallas Mavericks. LA scored ten points and collected seven rebounds. What was more amazing was that he limited Dirk to merely one field goal the entire fourth quarter of that game, similar to how he was able to limit Duncan's productivity using his length.

Although the Trailblazers were still struggling to win games, they did drastically improve from the previous year due to the additions of LA and Roy. Roy was an instant impact as a freshman player and was the best contender for the prize of top rookie. Aldridge was not bad either, given his limited minutes. When Joel Pryzbilla was sidelined due to injury sometime in February 2007, McMillan opted to insert LaMarcus into the starting lineup as the center. While starting for the Portland Trailblazers, LA averaged almost 15 points per game along with 8 boards a night.

Things took a turn for the worst for the young LaMarcus Aldridge in April 2007. He was diagnosed with Wolff-Parkinson-White Syndrome, a heart ailment that caused him shortness of breath. He would miss the rest of the games for the Blazers that season. At the end of his rookie campaign, LaMarcus Aldridge averaged 9 points per game, 5 rebounds, and 1.2 swats. He was named to the NBA All-Rookie First Team together with teammate Brandon Roy who won the Rookie of the Year honors.

Second Year

LaMarcus Aldridge's second year in the NBA would turn out to be his breakout year as a professional. The Portland Trailblazers traded their longtime starting power forward and leading scorer over to the New York Knicks for Steve Francis and Channing Frye during the 2007 NBA Draft. With Randolph gone, the starting power forward position was open for LA to take. Moreover, they also won the NBA Draft by having been able to get the number one overall pick. For the first overall pick of the 2008 NBA Draft, the Portland Trailblazers took standout college center Greg Oden because of his NBA-ready size and his defensive presence in the paint. The Blazers took Oden instead of the National Player of the Year Kevin Durant. This choice would be highly criticized in later years because Durant became a four-time scoring champion and an MVP.

With Aldridge, Oden, and reigning Rookie of the Year Brandon Roy, the Portland Trailblazers had a good and solid young trio to build around for the future of their franchise. The big and tall frontline of the Blazers with Aldridge and Oden would have done some serious damage in the NBA. In fact, Aldridge and Oden were both impressive in the Summer League and in pre-season games. However, Oden suffered a stress fracture in his knee and required micro-fracture surgery to repair it. The surgery required Oden to be sidelined the entire 2007-08 season and he did not even play a single minute in the regular season. The debut of Portland's twin towers would have to wait for another year.

Despite the setback, Portland became an early playoff contender with both Brandon Roy and LA playing well beyond what people had expected them to. Both sophomore players improved their play drastically, especially on the offensive end. Roy and Aldridge were Portland's designated go-to-guys because former team leading scorer Randolph was already with the Knicks. Brandon Roy rose to become the team's leading scorer while Aldridge was the second option. As a second option, Aldridge still flourished. He improved his offense and further honed his midrange and fadeaway jump shots that would prove to be his biggest weapons in his NBA career.

The Blazers were so good at one point in the season that they were able to win 13 straight games in December and had the best record for that month with 13 wins and two losses. Portland's success and the improved play of their duo made coaches turn their eye on the budding young stars of the Blazers. Brandon Roy was selected to play in his first All-Star appearance that season while Aldridge continued to play consistently on both ends.

At the end of the season, LaMarcus Aldridge's stats increased across the board. Playing as a starter, he averaged 35 minutes a game, 17.8 points per night, 7.6 rebounds an outing, and 1.2 blocks a game. His 17.8 points were second only to Brandon Roy on the team. His improved play together with the surprising play of the Blazers earned LaMarcus several votes for the Most Improved Player award. LA finished third in voting for that accolade, however. The Portland Trailblazers improved to a record of 41 wins to 41 losses. Despite the improved team record, the Trailblazers missed the playoffs that season.

Continued Consistency

Aldridge played with the same consistent offense and dependable defense in his third year in the NBA and with the Portland Trailblazers. With LA and Roy continuing to lead the Blazers in the duo's third season together, the Blazers would become one of the best teams in the Western Conference. Of course, the duo could not have carried Portland on their own. The Blazers added more talent via the NBA Draft. They drafted two of the best international players available in the draft. First up was wingman Rudy Fernandez, who played very well for the Spanish Men's Basketball Team in the 2008 Olympic Games. The second international player was young Frenchman Nicolas Batum. With all their offseason additions, the best part was still that Greg Oden was already available to play in his official rookie season in the NBA.

With Greg Oden back in the lineup, the Blazers would have a solid frontcourt tandem. However, Nate McMillan opted not to start Oden for various reasons. Firstly, he did not want to force Oden back to the rigors of an NBA game since he just got back from an injury. Secondly, Joel Pryzbilla handled himself well as a starter. And third, McMillan did not want to make Aldridge feel like he was the third option on the starting lineup. Despite Aldridge being the "second option" on the team, he struggled at the start of the season due to having to adjust with Oden on the floor. However, LA would return back to form a month or so into the 2008-09 NBA season.

The Trailblazers continued to rise to the top of the rankings in the Western Conference. Both Roy and

Aldridge played consistently and actually improved from their sophomore year. Brandon Roy was selected to play in his second straight All-Star game and was also named to the All-NBA Second Team at the end of the season. Their sweet-shooting rookie Rudy Fernandez also appeared in the midseason celebration as a contestant in the Slam Dunk contest. In that season, Fernandez set a record for most three-point shots made by a rookie. Meanwhile, Greg Oden played 61 games as a rookie while starting 39 of them. On the other hand, LaMarcus Aldridge was without any individual accolades or broken NBA records, but was happy and content with how the Blazers improved as a team. The Portland Trailblazers finished the 2008-09 season with a 54-28 record, which was good enough for the fourth seed in the West, a drastic improvement from previous years. Aldridge averaged 18.1 points per game, 7.5 rebounds a night, and 1 block per outing in his third season.

For the first time since the 2003 playoffs, the Portland Trailblazers made the postseason. What was impressive was that they jumped from being a non-contender to the fourth seed in the Western Conference and had home court advantage in the first round. The Blazers were set to face the Houston Rockets, who were without their star wingman Tracy McGrady. Nevertheless, the towering 7'6" Yao Ming shadowed the paint for the Rockets and proved to be literally the biggest thorn in the side of the Trailblazers.

Despite the excitement of returning to the playoffs and with the home court advantage at that, the Portland Trailblazers would lose game one at home in a blowout loss to the Rockets. Yao Ming dominated the paint with 24 points. Neither Pryzbilla nor Oden could stop the bigger Yao. On the other hand, Roy led the Blazers with 21 points. But the biggest glare for the Blazers was that LaMarcus Aldridge was limited to 7 points on 3 out of 12 shooting from the field. Worse,

LA could not stop Argentinian power forward Luis Scola from scoring 19 points on the offensive end.

The Rockets may have stolen home court advantage away from the Trailblazers, but Portland would not allow them to take two games in the Moda Center. Both Brandon Roy and LaMarcus Aldridge refused to lose once again when they exploded for a combined 69 points. LaMarcus broke out from his game one slump and scored 27 points on 11 of 19 shooting and grabbed 12 rebounds. Even more impressive was his partner Brandon Roy. Roy recorded his career playoff high with 42 points. On the defensive end, Pryzbilla held Yao Ming to only 11 points. The effort of the Blazer duo earned Portland the tight win against a gritty Rockets team.

When the series shifted over to Houston for game three, the Rockets would regain control over the series by beating the Trailblazers in a tight 86 to 83 win. Aldridge would again struggle to contain the Argentinian post scorer. Luis Scola recorded 19 points on 8 out of 15 shooting. He won out his match-up with Aldridge who only had 13 points on 6 out of 15 shooting. Roy led the way again for Portland with 19 followed by the 17 points off the bench by Rudy Fernandez.

In game four, the Houston Rockets gripped the series firmly in their hands with a victory at their home court to push themselves to a 3-1 lead over the Portland Trailblazers. Yao Ming broke out of his two-game scoring slump by putting up 21 points and grabbing 12 rebounds. Roy led the Blazers with 31 points followed by the 19 points of LA. Despite the Blazer duo's solid performance, they still fell to a one-point loss to the Rockets in a low-scoring 89 to 88 game.

The Houston Rockets were only one win away from proceeding to the second round and from eliminating the young and inexperienced Portland Trailblazers. Though unhardened in the playoffs, the Blazers would chase off eliminations by leaning on their two best players. Both Aldridge and Roy scored 25 points in their home floor on an 11-point victory. Meanwhile, Scola scored well against the defense of Aldridge by dropping 21 points on a solid 10 of 13 shooting from the floor.

Portland's inexperience in the playoffs would prove to be their downfall in game six. The Houston Rockets played a very good second quarter offensively and defensively to finally dispatch the young Trailblazers squad in a 92-76 blowout victory. Ron Artest used all of his veteran smarts to lead the Rocket points. Yao followed suit with 17 points and 10 boards. The Portland duo played extremely well. LaMarcus had 26 points while Roy had 22 of his own. However, none of the other Blazers were able to contribute to the cause. The other three starters scored a combined seven points while the bench only had 21 points. Despite the inexperience, the Blazers proved that they were good enough to get to the playoffs. The series loss to the Rockets is what we could call as a growing pain for LaMarcus and his young squad.

Coming into the 2009-10 NBA season, LaMarcus Aldridge earned a five-year contract extension worth $65 million. His counterpart in the backcourt Brandon Roy also received an extension with the same length. The Trailblazers still played with the same kind of intensity that had them contending for a playoffs squad the previous year. However, they started the season with a depleted lineup due to injuries to Rudy Fernandez and Nicolas Batum. LA and Brandon also played through injuries of their own. Nevertheless, they still remained competitive due to several key offseason acquisition Andre Miller running the offense effectively.

The Portland Trailblazers' luck would not turn out for the better. Greg Oden suffered another season-ending knee injury early in December. The former number one overall pick could not stay healthy to get some traction in what would have been a great NBA career. Adding more problems to the Blazers' depth at the center position, Joel Pryzbilla also suffered a season-ending knee injury. This forced Nate McMillan, who was also injured at one point in the season, to play Aldridge at center in some stretches, especially when the 36-year old Juwan Howard was out there staring.

Because of the huge hole at the center position for the Trailblazers, the team traded for 35-year old veteran center Marcus Camby in exchange for back-up guard Steve Blake. With Camby in the paint for the Blazers, LA was back to playing the power forward position to spot up for midrange jumpers. With Oden gone, Aldridge was having more touches on the offensive end, especially because Camby was not a threat at that end of the court. He also played more minutes at 37.5 per game. At the season's end, Aldridge averaged 17.9 and 8 rebounds per game. Despite playing with the same kind of consistency he has played with over the last three seasons, he still failed to get the All-Star attention he deserved. Meanwhile, the other half of the duo, Brandon Roy, was named as an All-Star for the third straight season. Roy would end the regular season early to repair a slight meniscus tear. Despite having an injury-plagued season, the Trailblazers had a 50-32 regular season record and were 6th place in the very competitive Western Conference.

The Trailblazers would start the first round of the playoffs against the Phoenix Suns. The Suns were a rejuvenated run-and-gun team with two-time MVP Steve Nash running the point together with scorer Jason Richardson and athletic big man Amare Stoudemire. Without Brandon Roy to start the playoffs, the Blazers would have to lean on their skillful big man LaMarcus Aldridge and on veteran point guard Andre Miller for leadership and scoring.

Leaning on the strengths of their veterans, the Portland Trailblazers managed to steal a road game in Phoenix to gain control of home court advantage and of the series. Miller led the way for the Blazers with 31 points. The biggest story though was how the 35-year old center Camby helped to alleviate the defensive burden away from LA by defending Stoudemire very well. Camby finished the game with 17 rebounds and three blocks. Aldridge played well with 22 points, but only had three rebounds. Nash led the Suns with 25 points and 9 assists.

The injury bug still found its way to haunt the Trailblazers in the playoffs. They would lose Nicolas in the middle of the game to a shoulder injury. Furthermore, the Suns played terrific defense on the only other scorer that the Blazers had, aside from LaMarcus Aldridge. Veteran forward Grant Hill was assigned to cover Miller and the old point guard could not muster to score as much as he did the previous game. Meanwhile, Aldridge only had 11 points on 3 out of 8 shooting from the floor for the Blazers who lost by 29 points in game two.

The series shifted over to Portland for game three. The Trailblazers had already done their job by stealing a game in Phoenix. All they had to do was defend their home court for two consecutive games. It turned out they could not do so. Jason Richardson exploded for

42 points on 8-12 shooting from three-point territory. The Blazers had no answer for the hot-shooting wingman and they lost again in blowout fashion. Aldridge scored 17 points on another dismal 5 out of 14 shooting from the floor. Meanwhile, Batum only played 9 minutes due to the injury he suffered the previous game. With the win on game three, the Suns regained home court advantage and led the series for the first time.

The Trailblazers suddenly turned their luck around in game four. Their three-time All-Star shooting guard returned from his surgery to give new life to his team. Though Brandon Roy only mustered to score 10 points off the bench, it was the inspiration he gave to the home crowd and to his team that proved to be the most instrumental. LaMarcus Aldridge suddenly woke up from his two-game shooting slump to score 31 points and grab 11 rebounds. He was 11 out of 19 from the floor. Stoudemire led the game for the Suns with 26 points. The series was now tied at two wins apiece.

Back in Phoenix, the Suns bench suddenly exploded for 55 points to secure a 107-88 win. The former Blazer Channing Frye had 20 points, Jared Dudley scored 19, and Goran Dragic recorded 7. The Blazers' bench could not match their counterparts in terms of scoring. Roy only had 5 points off the bench in his second game back from his injury. Miller led Portland with 21 points while Aldridge had 17, but could only muster to get 2 rebounds, despite his size and length. In game six in Portland, the Blazers tried to rally for a win, but just fell short. They ultimately lost the game 90 to 99 and the series 2 to 4. Aldridge had 16 points and Webster, off the bench, scored 19. Richardson led the Suns with 28 points. In the end, the Portland Trailblazers were just too inexperienced and too injured to give a strong fight to the Phoenix Suns.

Rise to All-Star Status

The 2010-11 Status would be a defining year for both LaMarcus Aldridge and the Trailblazers. With

Brandon Roy struggling to get healthy in their postseason matchup against the Suns, the Trailblazers signed promising second year wingman Wesley Matthews to a 5-year deal as insurance in case Roy would not be able to get back to All-Star status quickly. True enough, Brandon Roy struggled to stay healthy the early in the season and he was that he was going to be shut down indefinitely due to his chronic knee injuries. Adding more to the injured list was Greg Oden who would once again miss a full season to undergo micro fracture surgery on his left knee. Among the Trailblazers' projected trio of franchise superstars, only LaMarcus remained healthy.

With Brandon Roy out indefinitely, LaMarcus Aldridge became the focal point and the first option on offense. Both LA's touches and minutes increased due to the Blazers' lack of any other offensive option. It was Wesley Matthews who provided the scoring punch as the second option behind LA. He did well filling in for Roy, but could not replicate the same numbers and intangibles that Brandon provided for his team. And in the middle of the season, the Trailblazers sought to get help for Aldridge by trading for Charlotte Bobcats' forward Gerald Wallace in exchange for Joel Pryzbilla and Sean Marks. Wallace provided the Blazers with energy on the floor with his scoring, rebounding, and defense.

Aldridge almost singlehandedly brought Portland to playoff contention the entire season, and he posted career numbers while doing it. Even when Roy returned to the lineup, it was Aldridge leading the team both on and off the court. It was in the 2010-11 season where he scored a career high of 42 points. He was also Player of the Week several times that season for the Western Conference due to his ability to lead the Blazers on his own. Because of LaMarcus' stellar play that season, Trailblazers fans began a movement they called, "Send LA to LA," which was aimed at coaches to vote LaMarcus (LA) to the All-Star Team to be held in Los Angeles (LA). Despite the clamor of the fans and Aldridge's impressive numbers, the coaches did not select him as a part of the Western Conference All-Stars.

Although Aldridge did not become an All-Star that season, he posted then-career highs in both scoring and in rebounding. His numbers were very much All-Star material, and were even better than some of the other players who made it into the midseason classic. LA averaged 21.8 points per game and 8.8 rebounds per game that season. For the second time in his career, Aldridge was a contender for the Most Improved Player award, but finished second to Minnesota Timberwolves forward Kevin Love. Nevertheless, LaMarcus was given credit at the end of the season by getting selected into the All-NBA Third Team, the first major individual accolade in his career. With his leadership, the Blazers finished sixth in the West with a record of 48 wins and 34 losses.

The Trailblazers were set to face the third-seeded Dallas Mavericks in the playoffs. Veterans Dirk

Nowitzki, Jason Kidd, and Jason Terry, who were all hungry for an NBA title, led the Mavs. This was the postseason wherein Dirk Nowitzki would play out of his mind the entire playoffs. The Blazers were not spared of Dirk's crazy offensive play in the first round. It was going to be a classic matchup between Dirk and LaMarcus, two of the league's best power forwards.

The Mavericks' veterans made their intentions to go for a title run known in game one. Nowitzki dueled it out with Aldridge and scored 28 points. Jason Kidd scored 24 of his own, including six three-pointers. LA chipped in with 27 points of his own for the Blazers, who actually led by six in the middle of the fourth quarter. It was Dirk's terrific run in the final quarter that got the Mavs the win. Dirk was even better in game two. He scored 33 points to lead all Mavericks in scoring. Once again, the veterans stepped up. Kidd had 18 while Peja Stojakovic had 21 points that included several three-pointers to give the Mavs the momentum and the 101-88 victory. Aldridge had 24 points and 10 rebounds in game two.

The Blazers failed to steal one game in the Mavericks home court. When they went home for game three, it was their turn to defend their floor. Wesley Matthews started the game strong by scoring 22 in the first half. By the fourth quarter, the Trailblazers actually held a 13-point lead, but that lead was quickly trimmed down to 3 in the dying minutes. If it weren't for Andre Miller's clutch free throws, the Mavs would have made the game closer. In the end, Portland defended their first home game in the first round. Matthews had 25 while Aldridge scored 20. Dirk had another solid outing with 25 points while spitfire guard Jason Terry had 29 off the bench.

In game four, the Blazers rallied to an inspiring performance by the team's depleted former All-Star guard Brandon Roy. Roy scored 18 of his 24 points in the fourth quarter to lead the Trailblazers to a tight 84-82 victory. The Mavericks actually had an 18-point lead going into the fourth quarter and were looking to steal a game in Portland. Roy did not allow the Mavericks to take them down on their own home floor. He scored 18 out of the Blazers' 35 points in the fourth quarter, and actually hit a bank shot in the dying seconds to secure the lead and the victory for his team. Back in Dallas for game five, the Blazers would struggle the entire second half after a good start to the first quarter. The Mavericks would not allow the Trailblazers to mount another run like they did in the previous game. Once again, Aldridge struggled to contain the big German. Dirk Nowitzki scored 25. Aldridge had a subpar 6 out of 15 shooting for 12 points. Andre Miller led Portland with 18 points and Brandon Roy only had five, which was 19 points shy of his previous performance. The Blazers fell to a 2-3 series deficit. They were one loss away from elimination and needed to win the next game to force a deciding seventh game.

In Portland for game six, the Blazers started the first quarter off strong and had an eight-point lead. They would melt down in the second quarter when the Trailblazer bench could not match the productivity and experience of Dallas' second unit. Jason Terry scored 22 off the bench for the Mavericks who won the game 103 to 96. Dirk Nowitzki scored a game-high 33 points and 11 rebounds. The Blazers were top scored by Gerald Wallace's 32 points followed by the 25 of LA. Their production would prove to be for naught because they would play their final playoff game for the season. Aldridge averaged 20.8 points and 7.5 rebounds in the postseason. For the third straight year, the Portland Trailblazers would bow out of the first round of the playoffs.

The NBA went into a lockout after the 2010-11 season. It was not until December that the lockout ended and that teams were able to start training camp and the NBA regular season was shortened to a compressed 65 games. The long break would have benefited the injured Blazer duo of Brandon Roy and Greg Oden. Portland fans would have wanted their beloved trio to be healthy enough to finally play a full season together. However, Brandon Roy could not recover from his chronic knee injuries. In a move that would break the heart of Blazer hopefuls and basketball fans alike, Brandon Roy would retire as a three-time All-Star. For Oden's part, he still struggled to stay healthy and had to undergo another surgery to his knee. During the offseason, Andre Miller and Rudy Fernandez were both traded to the Dallas Mavericks in exchange for Raymond Felton. It would seem that the Blazers were trying to move on from Brandon Roy and Greg Oden to focus more on rebuilding around LaMarcus Aldridge. They also signed capable scorer Jamal Crawford to a one-year deal in order to fill the void that Roy and Fernandez had left.

Despite their offseason moves to fill in for Oden and Roy, the Blazers struggled to win the majority of their games. Aldridge would remain as the focal point of the offense, but they struggled to get consistent play from Wesley Matthews, Jamal Crawford, and Raymond Felton, who all may have suffered from the long layoff induced by the lockout. Because of the inconsistencies of the team's other players, Aldridge lacked a reliable second option to go to whenever he would struggle or get doubled up on.

Because of the team's struggles, head coach Nate McMillan was relieved of his duties after leading the team to three straight playoff appearances that all ended in the first round. The young assistant Kaleb Canales took over the team on an interim basis. Another midseason move that proved to be a game changer was when the team signed J.J. Hickson off the waivers when the Sacramento King waived him from their team. Hickson was an undersized center, but he was the reliever for the aging Marcus Camby, who was traded for Hasheem Thabeet, and he also prevented Aldridge from playing center, which he was not very fond of. The 2011-12 season was also the best year yet for French forward Nicolas Batum. Batum filled out the wing spot when Gerald Wallace was traded midseason to the New Jersey (now Brooklyn) Nets in exchange for a protected first round pick and for two role players. Oden was also released from the Trailblazers lineup after having only played a total of 82 games after five seasons.

Aldridge would, however, remain to play at an All-Star caliber level the entire season. Finally, LaMarcus was chosen to be an All-Star reserve for the Western Conference team for the first time in his career. It was a long overdue appreciation of LA's skills, work ethic, and role as the Blazers' top player. In his first All-Star game, Aldridge scored four points in only 9 minutes of play.

LaMarcus increased his play despite having no consistent second option. At the end of the season, he shot his best ever percentage from the floor with 51.2% and also shot a then-career high from the free throw line with 81.4%. Over the season, he averaged

21.7 points, 8.0 rebounds, 2.4 assists, and .8 blocks per game. However, LaMarcus could not lead his team to a playoff appearance, especially not with their dismal 28-win and 38-loss record.

Being the Franchise Player and the Coming of Damian Lillard

LaMarcus had undoubtedly been the face of the franchise since the 2010-11 season when the Blazers lost Roy and Oden. All the moves and acquisitions they would make from there on would have to be centered around LA's strengths on the floor and on his ability to lead a team. The team had holdovers Wes Matthews and JJ Hickson, who both played well as backup plans for Brandon Roy and Greg Oden. Nicolas Batum also started to play very well after he was inserted into the starting lineup following the Gerald Wallace trade. This was a core the Blazers were willing to build on, especially after Raymond

Felton and Jamal Crawford could not play effectively during their stint with Portland.

Coming into the 2012 offseason, the Gerald Wallace trade immediately paid dividends for the Trailblazer franchise. They ended up with the sixth overall pick for the 2012 NBA Draft and also had the 11th choice due to their bad record the previous season. For their first pick, they drafted Damian Lillard, a good scoring fourth year guard out of Weber State. For the 11th pick, they drafted 7'1" center Meyers Leonard who had a shooting touch that could extend to the three-point line. They also signed two draft picks from previous years, namely Victor Claver and Joel Freeland. Finally, Terry Stotts from the Dallas Mavericks was named as the head coach for the team after Canales took over on an interim basis.

LaMarcus Aldridge remained as the first option and the best player for the Portland Trailblazers. Nobody expected Damian Lillard to make the impact that he did in his rookie season. Lillard, who won MVP honors in the Summer League, provided what Aldridge has been looking for the past two seasons—a good second option. Lillard showed the poise and experience of someone playing beyond his years. He had a good shooting touch from three-point range, was very quick to penetrate inside, and could create plays effectively for his teammates. Lillard was undoubtedly the best rookie that season, and he lifted a lot of scoring burden from Aldridge. Nicola Batum also continued to improve. He became a better shooter, a better defender, and surprisingly, a better playmaker.

With Lillard and Batum helping out on the offense and with Wesley Matthews finally regaining his shooting touch, LA focused more on scoring inside and on grabbing rebounds. Aldridge was once again selected to be an All-Star for the West team. In his second All-Star appearance, LA played 11 minutes, but did not score on two field goal attempts for the West. He did have two blocks, however.

At the end of the 2012-13 season, LaMarcus Aldridge averaged 21.1 points per game, then-career highs of 9.1 rebounds per game and 2.6 assists per game, and 1.2 blocks per game. His new scoring partner Damian Lillard averaged 19 points per game and 6.5 assists per game. Lillard went on to unanimously win the Rookie of the Year award. He was only the fourth player after Ralph Sampson, David Robinson, and Blake Griffin to win Rookie of the Year unanimously. Despite having a new dynamic duo that both played very well, the Trailblazers failed to make a playoff seeding for the second straight season due to a 33-49 win-loss record.

The lack of success with the Portland Trailblazers weighed on LaMarcus Aldridge during the 2013 offseason. Aldridge had made the playoffs three times in his career with the Blazers, but he always lucked out of the first round. In the three other years with the team, he failed to make the playoffs with dismal win-loss records. Because of this, trade rumors began to circle around LaMarcus Aldridge and the Portland

Trailblazers. People began to speculate that he was unhappy with the state of the team, especially with their lack of postseason appearances and successes. Rumors suddenly circulated that Aldridge may have to demand a trade to get out of Portland or, if not, leave for free agency as soon as his contract was done. Aldridge assured the Portland faithful that he wanted to stay as a Blazer, but still wanted the team to improve their chances for an NBA title.

Giving in to their franchise player's wishes, the Portland Trailblazers front office added several capable players to bolster their lineup. First, they drafted scoring combo guard CJ McCollum out of Lehigh University with the 10th overall pick of the 2013 NBA Draft. They then signed 7-foot center Robin Lopez to relieve some defensive and rebounding burden from Aldridge. To strengthen their bench, they also signed veteran point guard and former All-Star Mo Williams to provide back up for Lillard.

Because of the additions and the improvements of several key players, the Trailblazers started the season on a very good note. At one point in November, they had an 11-game winning streak with Aldridge averaging 21.1 points and 11 rebounds in that stretch. Aldridge also had several memorable outputs in the 2013-14 season. He recorded 31 points and a career high 25 rebounds in a win over the Rockets. He was the first player in franchise history to have ever recorded a 30-25 in one game. He also established a new career high of 44 points against the Denver Nuggets. Because of his solid play, he was named Player of the Week and also earned a third straight Western Conference All-Star appearance. In what seemed to be a very long time since, the Trailblazers finally had two All-Stars in their team because reigning Rookie of the Year Damian Lillard was also named as an All-Star reserve, his first selection in a very young career. LA scored 4 points in the midseason classic while Damian had 9 in his All-Star debut.

With the two All-Stars playing out of their mind, the Blazers suddenly went back to playoff contention. The duo did not do it on their own, though. Wesley Matthews was playing at a career high level as well with 16 points per game and 2.5 three-pointers per game. Nicolas Batum was also rebounding and assisting at a career high pace with 7.5 and 5.1 respectively. Finally, Robin Lopez was playing at his career best with 11.1 points and 8.5 rebounds.

At the end of the season, LaMarcus Aldridge recorded season highs in both points and rebounds. He averaged 23.2 points per game and 11.1 rebounds per game. With his stellar play for the Blazers, he was named to the All-NBA Third Team for the second time in his career. His counterpart at the backcourt averaged 20.7 points a night and 5.6 assists per game. The strength of the Blazers team propelled their record to 54 wins and 28 losses, a 21-win improvement from the previous season. They earned the 5th seed in the ultra-competitive Western Conference.

The Blazers were now back in the NBA playoffs after a two-year absence from the postseason. In their last three playoff appearances, the Blazers and Aldridge exited early due to first round losses. Now back in the playoffs, Aldridge would not allow his team to lose in the first round once again. Standing in their way was the Houston Rockets led by the bearded high-scoring shooting guard James Harden along with his big buddy in the paint Dwight Howard. The Rockets had home court advantage with the 4th seed.

LaMarcus Aldridge immediately made his return to the playoffs known. He scored a career playoff high of 46 points in an overtime win of 122 to 120 in Houston, Texas. His 46 points were also a playoff franchise high for the Blazers. He also had 18 rebounds for the Blazers team that stole home court advantage from the Houston Rockets, who actually led by 11 with less than five minutes remaining in the fourth quarter.

Lillard also played terrifically with 31 points in his first career playoff game. Harden and Howard each had 27 for the Rockets.

LA followed up with an encore performance in game two. He once again scored at will with 43 points on 18 out 28 shooting from the field while playing merely 36 minutes. With his amazing performance, the Portland Trailblazers won the game 112 to 105 to take both of Houston's home games and take control over the series with two wins to nothing. Howard led the Rockets with 32 points and 15 rebounds.

The series moved over to Portland, Oregon for game three. The Blazers were looking to secure both wins at home to sweep the Houston Rockets out of the playoffs. However, the Rockets would take revenge for their two home losses. James Harden played out of his mind with 37 points, 9 rebounds, and 6 assists. But the story of the game was former D-League player Troy Daniels who sank three three-pointers including the go-ahead shot in the dying seconds of overtime to secure the 121-116 victory for Houston. LaMarcus Aldridge finally slowed down a bit with 23 points and 10 rebounds. Lillard top scored for the Blazers with 30 points.

The series lead for the Blazers was now down to merely one game. However, they still had home court advantage because of the two wins they had in Houston. With a win in game four, they took command of the series with a 3-1 lead. For the third time in the series, the game was hard-fought enough to go into overtime. Aldridge was once again stellar with 29 points and 10 rebounds. After game four, Aldridge became the first player to record 140 points and 45 rebounds in the first four playoffs games of the series. However, it was Wes Matthews who became the hero for the Blazers. He broke out of a shooting slump to score 23 points. The biggest play of the night for him was when he stole the ball from Patrick Beverly in the dying seconds to prevent the Rockets from closing the gap. The Blazers won 123 to 120. The bearded guard of Houston led them with 28 followed by Chandler Parsons' 26.

The Trailblazers were merely one game away from finally breaking out of the first round in what seemed like more than a decade. However, the Rockets would not allow them to just suddenly breeze pass them and onto the second round. Houston would extend the series to at least one more game by winning on their home court 108 to 98. Dwight had 22 rebounds and 14 boards. Jeremy Lin off the bench scored 21 points for the Rockets. For the Blazers, LaMarcus Aldridge suddenly fell back down to earth after playing out his body in the first four games of the series. He only scored 8 points. Matthews had another good game with 27 points. Lillard had 26 for the Blazers who were on their way home to hopefully get rid of the Rockets for good.

Game six in Portland was so tightly contested that all quarters, except the fourth, were only separated by one point for either team. With the game on the line and with the Rockets up 98 to 96, Damian Lillard caught an inbound pass near half court and shot it just as time expired. What transpired next broke the hearts of the Houston Rockets. The near half-court shot of Lillard found its way through the hoop and down the net to score an immaculate 99 to 98 victory for the Portland Trailblazers. Lillard had 25 total points while Aldridge had 30 points and 13 rebounds. With the amazing buzzer-beater, the Portland Trailblazers were now on their way to the second round. For the first time in his career, Aldridge did not exit the first round of the playoffs.

The Portland Trailblazers were still on cloud nine over that Damian Lillard shot. They immediately went back to business because they were going to face the top-seeded San Antonio Spurs in the second round. The Spurs were peaking at the right time, they were in the mood, and in the right form to win a championship that season. Despite being led by their usual big three of Tim Duncan, Tony Parker, and Manu Ginobili, they were an extremely balanced team with a combination of old veterans and young talent, especially Kawhi Leonard. The Blazers were in for a rough one in the second round.

Come game one, the Spurs did not relent. They immediately gave the fight to the Trailblazers in the first half. They led by 25 coming into the fourth quarter and Portland could not fight back. Tony Parker ran roughshod over the defense of Damian Lillard by scoring a game high 33 points and assisting on 9 baskets. LaMarcus Aldridge had 32 of his own, but lacked help versus the balanced offense and great ball movement of the Spurs.

In game two, it was more of the same for the far more experienced San Antonio squad. They again built a huge lead as early as the first half with their terrific ball movement and balanced attack to win another blowout victory. Seven Spurs were in double digits led by the 20 points of Kawhi Leonard. The younger and inexperienced Trailblazers looked helpless once again.

Aldridge was defended very well by his childhood idol. He shot a horrific 6 out of 23 from the field for only 16 points. Damian Lillard didn't shoot that well either, going 8 out of 20 for 19 points of his own.

Back in Portland for game three, the Portland Trailblazers were looking to even up the score by winning both games. The Spurs' experience still triumphed over the home crowd of the Blazers, though. They started the first half very strong yet again to build another big lead that they would more or less sustain until the end of the game. The Spurs did not miss a single free throw out of their 25 attempts the entire game, and Tony Parker scored 20 of his 29 in the first half. Aldridge and Lillard both had 21 points and all of the Blazers starters scored in double digits with four of them scoring over 20. The glaring part was that the bench only had a total of six points the entire game versus the 40 San Antonio bench points.

Coming into game four, Portland was down 0-3 in the series. No team in NBA history has ever come back to win from a 0-3 deficit in a seven-game series. The Blazers fought back hard in game four, but only to prevent a sweep. The Trailblazers led the game for about 46 minutes the entire duration to prevent the Spurs from sweeping them and to extend the series to at least one more game. LaMarcus Aldridge had 19 points while Damian Lillard had 25. Nicolas Batum came up big with 14 points, 14 rebounds, and 8 assists for the Blazers team that survived one more game. The Spurs, after starting each game strong, struggled a bit to score. Parker only had 14 points to top score for his team.

The Trailblazers would not be spared from the destiny that befalls all teams that have trailed 0-3 in the playoffs. Kawhi Leonard and Danny Green both shot lights out from three-point territory and both scored 22 to beat the Portland Trailblazers, despite losing Tony Parker in the first half due to injury. After a tied first quarter, the Spurs won all three subsequent quarters to secure a 22-point victory over the less experienced

Portland Trailblazers. LaMarcus top scored for the Blazers with 21 points but could not do enough to stop the Spurs from going to the Western Conference Finals. In the end, LaMarcus Aldridge still fell short of an NBA title, or at least an appearance in the Finals despite finally being able to get past the first round. He did, however, have the best postseason numbers of his career with 26.2 points and 10.6 rebounds. His numbers were compounded by his phenomenal scoring output in their first round encounter against the Rockets. Though he still played his usual regular season numbers against the Spurs, it was not enough to slay the mighty kings of the Western Conference. The 2013-14 postseason would be the best and deepest playoffs run that Aldridge would have, even to this day.

Final Year with the Trailblazers

The Trailblazers, after a good postseason run the previous season, kept their starting core intact for the 2014-15 season. They bolstered the bench by signing veterans center Chris Kaman and point guard Steve Blake in the offseason. The Blazers once again started the season strong by winning nine straight games in November. At that point, it was as if Wesley Matthews could not miss from three-point range and the Blazers were working on all cylinders during that streak. Once again, it was their dynamic duo that led them in scoring.

LaMarcus played fantastically once again in what would be his final year with the Portland Trailblazers. In December, he became the second highest scorer in franchise history after passing Terry Porter. He began to norm 23 points and 10 rebounds throughout the first half of the season. Much like in LA's early years with the Blazers, the injury bug bit them hard once again. Robin Lopez suffered a fractured hand in December and had to sit out the next 23 games. LaMarcus was not spared from injuries, either. In January, he would tear a ligament in his thumb and would require surgery to fix it. The surgery needed him to be sidelined for two months, maximum. Being the fighter that Aldridge has always been, he opted not to get surgery until the season ended. He knew that the Blazers needed him in the lineup, even if he wasn't at his best because he was the team's leader and best player. He would only miss two games to rest that injury. However, the injury proved to have bothered him as he shot about 46% from the floor in the season, the lowest shooting percentage of his career.

Even though Aldridge was a virtual 20-10 guy during the majority of the season, he initially failed to make the Western Conference All-Stars starters. However, with the All-Star Anthony Davis of the New Orleans Pelicans injured, LA was chosen as the replacement for Davis in the starting lineup. Thus, LaMarcus was an All-Star for the fourth straight time in his career and an All-Star starter for the first time. He also had his best All-Star game outing with 18 points in only 18 minutes of playing time as a starter.

Aldridge was not done climbing up the records ladder. In March, LA became the Blazers' all-time leading rebounder in franchise history. Again, the injury bug bit and caused great damage to the already depleted Portland Trailblazers. Wesley Matthews tore his Achilles tendon in March. The injury required Matthews to miss the entire remainder of the season including the playoffs. Luckily, the Blazers were able to make a move earlier in February to get Arron Afflalo, a very capable defensive shooting guard. Afflalo had to fill in for the injured Wes Matthews. Afflalo could not replicate the scoring abilities of Matthews though, and it proved to be detrimental for the Blazers.

At the end of the 2014-15 regular season, LaMarcus Aldridge had a career high in points per game. He averaged 23.4 points per game to go along with 10.2 rebounds a night and 1 block per outing. He was recognized for his terrific performance the entire season as one of the 10 best players in the NBA that year when he earned a spot in the All-NBA Second Team. He also led the Trailblazers to become the fourth seed in the West with a 51-31 win-loss record. With the fourth seed, the Blazers had home court advantage against the Memphis Grizzlies in the first round.

The Memphis Grizzlies quickly negated the Blazers' home court advantage by winning in game one. It was a tough loss 86-100 for the Trailblazers against a physical defensive team. LaMarcus Aldridge had 32 points and 14 rebounds but his team never led against the very tough Memphis squad. Beno Udrih off the bench top scored for Memphis with 20 points while their frontcourt tandem of Randolph and Gasol had double-doubles of their own.

It was more of the same in game two. The Portland Trailblazers struggled against the tough defense of the Memphis Grizzlies, especially with the injuries they sustained to their core players. Aldridge was yet again a one-man crew by scoring 24 points and grabbing 14 boards. He could not do enough to stop the Grizzlies from grabbing two games away from their home court with an 82-97 victory.

By losing two games in Portland, the Trailblazers were in danger of getting swept because the series shifted over to Memphis for games three and four. They had to steal two games in Memphis to even up the series and to keep their postseason run alive. Despite the injury to Mike Conley, the Trailblazers could not stop the rampaging Grizzlies. Zach Randolph and Marc Gasol wreaked havoc inside the paint and were too tough to defend for the Blazer frontcourt. Nicolas Batum top scored for Portland with 27 points followed by the 26 of CJ McCollum off the bench. Aldridge had 21 points on 6 out of 18 shooting over the tough defense of Marc Gasol.

For the second time in less than a year, the Portland Trailblazers found themselves in another 0-3 playoffs deficit. They could not climb out of the hole the last time they found themselves in that situation. Could they finally come back to win it all? The Blazers tried to do so by winning game four in Memphis in a tough contested 99-92 battle. They managed to stave off elimination and would want to fully come back to win it all. Damian Lillard erupted for 32 points while LaMarcus Aldridge had 18 points and 12 rebounds. Marc Gasol led his Grizzlies with 21 points. Portland extended the series to at least one more game, but it was only one more game, unfortunately.

The Portland Trailblazers finally bowed out of the playoffs when the Grizzlies dispatched them on their own home court. The Blazers fought valiantly, but could not stop the Memphis frontcourt duo from imposing their will. Meanwhile, Aldridge struggled the entire game on a 5 out of 18 shooting for 14 points. The only bright spot for the Blazers was CJ McCollum off the bench with 33 points in a losing effort. The Grizzlies were on their way to the second round while the Blazers were sent away to go fishing.

LaMarcus Aldridge yet again bowed out early in the playoffs. Though norming 21.8 points per game and 11.2 rebounds in five games in the playoffs, Aldridge could not do what it took to get to the next round. In his five playoffs appearances, LA has only made out of the first round one time. With Aldridge struggling to get postseason success in Blazers uniform, people began to speculate whether the game five loss to the Grizzlies was going to be the last time LA would play for Portland since he was going to be a free agent, the most coveted one, in the offseason. Indeed, it was his last game for the Trailblazers.

The Most Coveted Free Agent in 2015

LaMarcus Aldridge would enter the free agent market in 2015 after five unsuccessful playoff trips with the Portland Trailblazers. At that point in his career, Aldridge was one of the best power forwards in the game together with the likes of Anthony Davis and Blake Griffin. And with most NBA teams adopting the spacing game wherein four players will spread the floor with their outside shooting, LA was highly coveted because he could shoot midrange jumpers.

Several teams had the capacity to sign the highly coveted big man away from the Portland Trailblazers. The frontrunners were the San Antonio Spurs, the Los Angeles Lakers, his hometown Dallas Mavericks, the Phoenix Suns, and of course the Portland Trailblazers. The Blazers had the capacity to pay LA with $27 million more than any other team could. So any team seeking to sign Aldridge would have had to convince him not with cash, but with a possibility of winning a title.

Aldridge met twice with the Los Angeles Lakers. The Lakers were a rebuilding team and had a severely depleted and aging Kobe Bryant in the twilight of his career. They also had a young core with Jordan Clarkson, D'Angelo Russell, and Julius Randle. However, LA did not go to LA because he did not like how Kobe sold the Lakers to him. He would have had to play as a second choice to Kobe Bryant and did not like the makeup of the Lakers roster.

The Phoenix Suns, on the other hand, had a good team centered on young point guards Eric Bledsoe and Brandon Knight. The team was possibly too young and too inexperienced for Aldridge to instantly win an NBA title in a year or two, though. For his hometown of Dallas, the Mavericks had enough talent and the proper coaching to get Aldridge a possible title run. However, with Dirk as the established power forward, Aldridge would have had to play center or play from the bench for the Mavs. He flirted with the idea of coming home to Dallas, but when he flirted too long, the Mavs signed LA's former teammate Wesley Matthews to a deal that would have made it impossible for them to sign Aldridge to a lucrative contract.[xix]

Then there were the San Antonio Spurs. The Spurs had been the most consistent and the best franchise in the NBA since the late 90's. They were a great organization and focused a lot on player development, among other things. The Spurs also had an exceptional coaching staff headed by Gregg Popovich who had led the Spurs to five NBA championships since taking over in the 90's. The Spurs personified excellence and were always ready to win a title every year, especially with their core trio of Duncan, Parker, and Ginobili. If LA wanted to win an NBA title, the Spurs were the best team to do so with.

In the end, LaMarcus Aldridge chose to sign with the San Antonio Spurs for a five-year, $80 million contract, which was much less than what he would have earned had he chosen to stay with Portland.[xx] He joined a team with multiple championship experiences and a good young defensive minded player Kawhi Leonard. At 30 years old, Aldridge was at his peak and was not getting any younger. Had he chosen one of the rebuilding teams, it would have taken him several years to contend for a title. The Spurs were just the right team, especially with how well-balanced and well-coached they had always been. The best part for

LA was that he was going to play alongside his childhood idol Tim Duncan and to learn everything he needed to learn from arguably the best power forward in the history of the game.

By signing with the Spurs, LA effectively ended his run with the Portland Trailblazers, the team that had been his home for nine seasons. Had he stayed longer with Portland, he would have been the best player in franchise history. It was not to be though, especially when title aspirations were already at stake. In his nine seasons with the Blazers, Aldridge averaged 19.3 points per game and 8.4 rebounds per game. He was also the franchise's second best scorer and its best rebounder.

First Season as a Spur

When Aldridge moved over to the Spurs, the landscape of the Western Conference quickly changed. Everyone knew that the Spurs were a title contender year in and year out. With the addition of Aldridge to their lineup, they immediately became title favorites (along with the Warriors and the Cavs) from being title contenders. The Spurs were already strong and were always obviously a playoff shoe-in. The biggest effect of Aldridge's move to Texas was that the Portland Trailblazers immediately fell off from playoff contention with the loss of their franchise superstar. The Blazers, in the hopes of building a solid team to convince Aldridge to stay with them, lost Wesley Matthews, Nicolas Batum, and Robin Lopez due to offseason moves to try and strengthen their lineup and free up cap space. Aldridge had already chosen the Spurs though, and Portland was left with a mediocre team that would bank solely on Damian Lillard and partially on rising guard CJ McCollum.

LaMarcus Aldridge joined a San Antonio Spurs team that was loaded with championship experience and was always a threat at winning a title every season. At their twilight years, Duncan, Parker, and Ginobili were no longer the players they once were, but could still effectively lead the game at any given time. With several shooters like Danny Green and Patty Mills around the perimeter, LA would have enough space to work his offense. Best of all, Aldridge did not have to work on defense as much as he had to when reigning Defensive Player of the Year Kawhi Leonard is out there making life tough for perimeter players. From being a virtual do-it-all guy in Portland, LaMarcus now had tons of help to make life easier for him as a Spur.

The Spurs have always prided themselves with their terrific ball movement and balanced scoring effort. With Aldridge and Leonard in the lineup though, they were going to be the unofficial first options for the San Antonio Spurs. The coming of Aldridge made Popovich tweak their style a little bit. In the past four seasons, the Spurs were playing a fast-paced game that centralized on ball movement and outside shooting. Now, they transitioned back to their old style of a slow-paced defensive game, but still focused their offense on ball movement.

Aldridge made his debut for the Spurs in a game against the Oklahoma City Thunder. They would lose that game and Aldridge had a mediocre outing of 11 points and 5 rebounds. Early in the season in November 11, LA returned to Portland, his former home. Now with San Antonio, it was his first game against his former team. He played a solid game by scoring 23 points and 6 boards to win the game by double digits. As a Spur, Aldridge has been playing his lowest minutes since his rookie season, but still manages to put up solid numbers. He is currently averaging 15.8 points, 8.9 rebounds, and 1.2 blocks in 22 starts for San Antonio while playing only 29.5 minutes per game. With his addition to the team, the Spurs are currently one of the best teams in the league, second only to the Golden State Warriors in the win-loss column.

Chapter 5: LaMarcus Aldridge's Personal Life

LaMarcus Nurae Aldridge was born on July 19, 1985. He is currently 30 years of age. His parents are Marvin and Georgia Aldridge, who stand at 6'6" and 6'2", respectively. Marvin was an alcoholic during LaMarcus' childhood and was kicked out of the household during LA's teen years. Marvin and LaMarcus do not have a good relationship with each other. LA actually invited Marvin to be at his draft night on the condition that his father would be sober. Marvin failed to attend for unknown reasons. Meanwhile, his mother Georgia was always supportive of LaMarcus' basketball career, even going back to his teen years. She never let him become too obsessed with the game though, and always made sure he studied well. Because of that, LaMarcus Aldridge grew up to become a very exceptional student athlete in high school and in college.

LaMarcus has an older brother LaVontae Aldridge. He and LaVontae are six years apart. LaVontae is also a tall person standing at around 6'10". He was a former basketball star in high school and played competitively well in Howard Junior College. LaVontae was a very big influence on the basketball career of LA. He helped his younger brother to get better as a player, especially when the younger Aldridge struggled to learn the game at an early age. He pushed his brother to work on his game and instilled the basic fundamentals of footwork and anticipation on the defensive end.[xxi] LaMarcus also has a cousin named Marlon Hairston, who is playing competitive football with the Colorado Rapids.

LaMarcus credits a very large part of his basketball career to his high school coach, Robert Allen. Allen did not make life easy on the young LA. He forced him to improve his conditioning by having him run almost 9 miles whenever LA would become lazy during practices. Allen was responsible for making

Aldridge into a gym rat and a hard worker in improving his game. Had Allen not pushed LaMarcus to his limit every single day, Aldridge would probably had not become the NBA All-Star he is today and might not even have made it into the NBA.

LaMarcus Aldridge has two children with his ex-girlfriend. His first child is Jaylen Lea who was born in April 2009 and is currently six years old. LaMarcus Aldridge Jr. who was born in 2011 and is currently four years of age following Jaylen.

Chapter 6: Aldridge's Legacy and Future

Standing at nearly 7-feet tall with a 7'5" wingspan and weighing in at about 245 lbs., LaMarcus Aldridge has the height, length, and strength of a solid big man in the NBA. LA was not always about size alone though, because he was one of the best power forwards the NBA has seen in recent years. He has a complete offensive game and can score from anywhere on the floor. He probably has the best midrange game amongst all of the league's power forwards. He has a very good jump shot that utilizes more of his upper body than his legs. He shoots his jump shots so high above his head that it is virtually impossible to block them. Despite his solid play at the perimeter he also has the post play that can rival even the best centers in the league. His go-to-move at the low post is his seemingly impossible to guard turnaround jump shot that he releases just as high as his perimeter jumpers.

LA is also not too shabby defensively and has consistently blocked more than one shot per game in his entire career.

Aldridge may not have changed the game very much and was not a pioneer in his own right, but his style of play has been eerily similar to that of Tim Duncan and Kevin Garnett, two pioneers and two of the best power forwards to have ever played the game. Aldridge has continued to be the standard bearer for the same style of basketball that has made Duncan and Garnett into legendary players. He played with the same kind of fundamentality as those two legends and has made that kind of basketball still relevant in today's NBA game. With his midrange shooting, he has become an invaluable asset especially because teams have been transitioning to a more spacious game where most players, except the center, would camp out in the perimeter to space the floor.

With his superior skills on the offensive and capable defensive prowess, LaMarcus ranks up there among the best power forwards in the game today and rivals other transcendent players in the position like Blake Griffin, Anthony Davis, and Kevin Love. He may not be as athletic and as mobile as Griffin and Davis are, but he is the better player in terms of offensive fundamentals because of his consistent midrange game and his excellent post moves. His status as a perennial All-Star and as one of the best power forwards in the league catapulted him to become the most coveted free agent in the offseason of 2015.

When it comes right down to ranking some of the best Portland Trailblazers players, LaMarcus belongs way up in the upper echelon. He spent nine years in the Trailblazers franchise and turned the team around from being a cellar dweller to a Western Conference playoff contender. He was set to be one of the cornerstones of a trio of superstars that included Brandon Roy and Greg Oden. Brandon Roy enjoyed a short yet successful NBA career that was cut short by nagging knee injuries. Greg Oden never made much of an impact in the NBA and managed to only play 82 games for the Trailblazers. He would have been one of the best centers in the league, had he stayed healthy. Even without Roy and Oden, LaMarcus made the Blazers competitive year in and year out by carrying the load on his back.

LaMarcus has played his best years in Portland. It was there that he first became an NBA All-Star in 2012 at the age of 26. Prior to becoming an All-Star, he was consistently putting up nearly 20 points per game and nearly 10 rebounds a night. It took until his sixth season as a Blazer to be recognized as one of the top players in the NBA. As a Trailblazer, LaMarcus averaged a career total of nearly 20 points per game and nearly 9 rebounds a night. He finished his career in Portland as the second best scorer in Trailblazers history and as the franchise's top rebounder. He also played the fourth most games and the third most minutes in Blazers history and is also third in most career blocks. All those career achievements have made Aldridge arguably the second best Trailblazers player behind Clyde Drexler. Had he stayed longer with the Portland franchise, he would have played more games, scored more points, and grabbed more rebounds to become the best player to ever wear the Trailblazers uniform.

LaMarcus Aldridge has also become one of the centerpieces for the San Antonio Spurs team that might see two of its core trio of stars leave the game soon. Tim Duncan and Manu Ginobili will be retiring any time and that leaves Tony Parker as the only one left of the legendary Spurs big three. Aldridge will be the cornerstone for the Spurs in the coming seasons together with budding two-way player Kawhi Leonard. He and Leonard may fill in as the new pieces together with Parker to form another big three in San Antonio. San Antonio has a good roster filled with young talent and veteran players that would help transition the team into a new era. With how well the Spurs front office draft talented players and with their excellent way of developing talent, LaMarcus and Kawhi will soon lead their own Spurs team that could possibly make damage in the playoffs and win a title once again for San Antonio.

When he decided to play with the Spurs, many people began to think that Aldridge had become the heir-apparent for Tim Duncan in San Antonio. Tim Duncan is in the twilight years of his career, despite still playing at a very high level for his advanced age by NBA standards. It won't be too soon until he retires as one of the greatest NBA players in history and as the best player in Spurs history. With Aldridge now donning a Spur uniform, Tim Duncan may have found the person who plays the same kind of fundamental offensive game he has been playing since 1997. Duncan may now be able to retire knowing that Aldridge is there to pick up the reigns of the San Antonio Spurs franchise as soon as he retires. The best part for Aldridge is that he gets to play alongside and learn from arguably the best power forward in NBA history. Duncan has always been a perennial winner and always played at an MVP level. Aldridge will be lucky if Duncan will be able to instill at least half of what he knows. With Duncan as his mentor and with the excellent Spurs organizations backing him up, Aldridge may soon win an NBA title and may soon become of the of the best power forwards in the history of the NBA.

Final Word/About the Author

I was born and raised in Norwalk, Connecticut. Growing up, I could often be found spending many nights watching basketball, soccer, and football matches with my father in the family living room. I love sports and everything that sports can embody. I believe that sports are one of most genuine forms of competition, heart, and determination. I write my works to learn more about influential athletes in the hopes that from my writing, you the reader can walk away inspired to put in an equal if not greater amount of hard work and perseverance to pursue your goals. If you enjoyed *LaMarcus Aldridge: The Inspiring Story of One of Basketball's Most Dominant Power Forwards*, please leave a review! Also, you can read more of my works on *Colin Kaepernick, Aaron Rodgers, Peyton Manning, Tom Brady, Russell Wilson, Michael Jordan, LeBron James, Derrick Rose, Kevin Garnett, Paul George, Kyrie Irving, Klay Thompson,*

Stephen Curry, Kevin Durant, Russell Westbrook, Anthony Davis, Chris Paul, Blake Griffin, Kobe Bryant, Joakim Noah, Scottie Pippen, Carmelo Anthony, Kevin Love, Grant Hill, Tracy McGrady, Vince Carter, Patrick Ewing, Karl Malone, Tony Parker, Allen Iverson, Hakeem Olajuwon, Reggie Miller, Michael Carter-Williams, John Wall, James Harden, Tim Duncan, and *Steve Nash* in the Kindle Store. If you love basketball, check out my website at claytongeoffreys.com to join my exclusive list where I let you know about my latest books and give you lots of goodies.

Like what you read? Please leave a review!

I write because I love sharing the stories of influential people like LaMarcus Aldridge with fantastic readers like you. My readers inspire me to write more so please do not hesitate to let me know what you thought by leaving a review! If you love books on life, basketball, or productivity, check out my website at claytongeoffreys.com to join my exclusive list where I let you know about my latest books. Aside from being the first to hear about my latest releases, you can also download a free copy of *33 Life Lessons: Success Principles, Career Advice & Habits of Successful People*. See you there!

Clayton

References

[i] Shelmon, David. "Gregg Popovich says he 'begged' to bring in LaMarcus Aldridge". *Sports Outwest*. 7 November 2015. Web

[ii] "LaMarcus Aldridge". *Jock Biography*. Web

[iii] Thompson, Wayne. "LaMarcus Aldridge: Ridin' with the L-Train". *Rip City Magazine*. Web

[iv] Thompson, Wayne. "LaMarcus Aldridge: Ridin' with the L-Train". *Rip City Magazine*. Web

[v] Thompson, Wayne. "LaMarcus Aldridge: Ridin' with the L-Train". *Rip City Magazine*. Web

[vi] Thompson, Wayne. "LaMarcus Aldridge: Ridin' with the L-Train". *Rip City Magazine*. Web

[vii] Chan, Lorne, "Back to Texas: LaMarcus Aldridge". *NBA.com*. 10 July 2015. Web

[viii] Thompson, Wayne. "LaMarcus Aldridge: Ridin' with the L-Train". *Rip City Magazine*. Web

[ix] Chan, Lorne, "Back to Texas: LaMarcus Aldridge". *NBA.com*. 10 July 2015. Web

[x] Chan, Lorne, "Back to Texas: LaMarcus Aldridge". *NBA.com*. 10 July 2015. Web

[xi] "LaMarcus Aldridge". *NBA Draft*. Web

[xii] "LaMarcus Aldridge". *Draft Express*. Web

[xiii] "LaMarcus Aldridge". *Draft Express*. Web

[xiv] "LaMarcus Aldridge". *Draft Express*. Web

[xv] Tokito, Mike. "NBA High-5: Blazers-Raptors is chance to revisit LaMarcus Aldridge-Andrea Bargnani draft picks". *Oregon Live*. 2012 December 10, 2012. Web

[xvi] Ilika, Dan. "What if Aldridge Were a Raptor?". *Toronto Sun*. 11 February 2011. Web

[xvii] Thompson, Wayne. "LaMarcus Aldridge: Ridin' with the L-Train". *Rip City Magazine*. Web

[xviii] Thompson, Wayne. "LaMarcus Aldridge: Ridin' with the L-Train". *Rip City Magazine*. Web

[xix] Wojnarowski, Adrian. "Five days in free agency: Inside the courtship of LaMarcus Aldridge". *Yahoo Sports*. 11 November 2015. Web

[xx] McPherson, Steve. "NBA Free Agency: How the Spurs Swung LaMarcus Aldridge". *Rolling Stones Magazine*. 6 July 2015. Web

[xxi] "LaMarcus Aldridge". *Jock Biography*. Web

Printed in Great Britain
by Amazon